E PLURIBUS UNUM

BY THE PEOPLE

THE PRESIDENTIAL CABINET

Bill McAuliffe

Creative Education ★ Creative Paperbacks

TABLE OF CONTENTS

4

WE THE PEOPLE

REFERENCE

In the 1790s, running the United States government was a job full of surprises. No one had done it before.

THE PRESIDENTIAL CABINET

The highest officials were like the founders of modern companies who start out working by themselves in their garages. Edmund Randolph, the first attorney general of the U.S., was in such a position. He had to set up a government agency without any money from Congress. Randolph's job was to provide legal advice to the president and members of Congress. He also had to represent the government in cases before the Supreme Court. But to make ends meet, he took on private legal work. The next 21 attorneys general (until 1853) continued this practice of dual careers. Today, that wouldn't be allowed, since it could lead to many **conflicts of interest**. It's an example of how history and circumstance have drastically changed the roles of presidential cabinet members. It is also evidence of how those in office have changed to respond to the needs determined by the people.

Attorney General Randolph was among four officials in Washington's cabinet.

LINE OF PRESIDENTIAL SUCCESSION

PRESIDENT **VICE PRESIDENT** **SPEAKER OF THE HOUSE**

SECRETARY OF DEFENSE **SECRETARY OF THE TREASURY** **SECRETARY OF STATE** **PRESIDENT PRO TEMPORE OF THE SENATE**

ATTORNEY GENERAL **SECRETARY OF THE INTERIOR** **SECRETARY OF AGRICULTURE** **SECRETARY OF COMMERCE**

SECRETARY OF TRANSPORTATION **SECRETARY OF HOUSING AND URBAN DEVELOPMENT** **SECRETARY OF HEALTH AND HUMAN SERVICES** **SECRETARY OF LABOR**

SECRETARY OF ENERGY **SECRETARY OF EDUCATION** **SECRETARY OF VETERANS AFFAIRS** **SECRETARY OF HOMELAND SECURITY**

The **PRESIDENTIAL SUCCESSION ACT OF 1947** set the current order of succession.

CHAPTER 1

NOT IN THE INSTRUCTIONS

THE PRESIDENTIAL CABINET

There is not a word in the U.S. Constitution about the president's cabinet. Yet the 16 people in the cabinet today are among the most powerful in the U.S. They are in charge of the departments that make up the executive branch of the federal government. Appointed by the president and confirmed by the Senate, they meet regularly with the president and advise him or her on issues of war and peace, national security, the economy, health, schools, and the environment, among others. They supervise millions of workers and budgets in the billions of dollars. Like the vice president, who is also a cabinet member, they are each ranked in the line of **presidential succession**. Each person earns just under $200,000 per year. (That is half the president's salary.)

★ **Of the positions now in the presidential cabinet, only four ... have been there since the days of George Washington, the first president.** ★

NOT IN THE INSTRUCTIONS

The model for the presidential cabinet appears to have originated in 15th-century Britain. A group of advisers to the king met in the royal chambers. It was a space small enough to be called a "cabinet." They became known as the Cabinet Council.

Of the positions now in the presidential cabinet, only four (plus the vice president) have been there since the days of George Washington, the first president. These are the secretary of defense (then called the secretary of war), the secretary of the treasury, the secretary of state, and the attorney general. All were established within weeks of each other in August and September 1789. Many have been added, but some, like postmaster general, have been dropped. Other positions have been merged or split.

From Washington's war department have come separate secretaries of war, the navy, and air force. Those were merged into a single position in 1949. Today, the secretary of defense oversees a budget of nearly $700 billion. The Department of Defense (DOD) is also the largest employer in the U.S. It is headquartered in the world's largest office building, the Pentagon, in Arlington, Virginia.

The first cabinet-level department created in 1789 was the treasury. The new nation faced huge debts and uncertainty about money after the Revolution. How to manage its finances was of primary concern.

The loftiest cabinet position is secretary

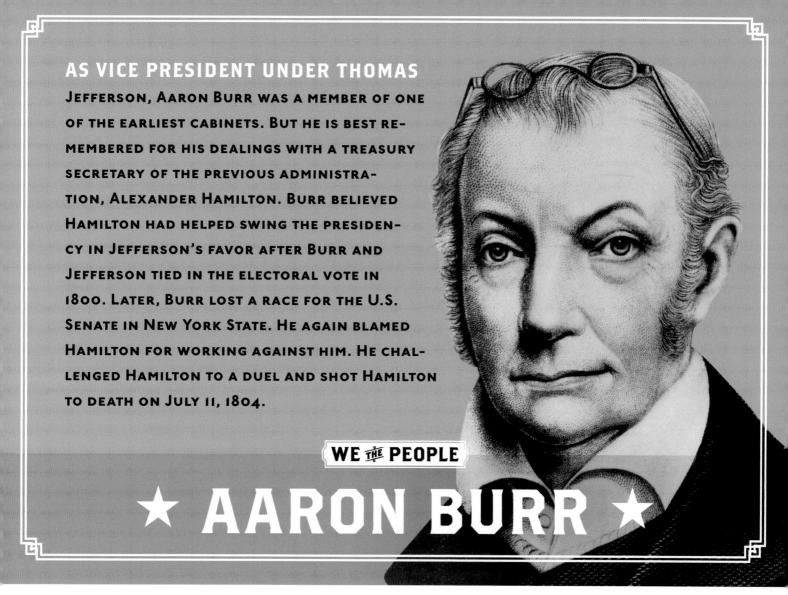

★ AARON BURR ★

AS VICE PRESIDENT UNDER THOMAS JEFFERSON, AARON BURR WAS A MEMBER OF ONE OF THE EARLIEST CABINETS. BUT HE IS BEST REMEMBERED FOR HIS DEALINGS WITH A TREASURY SECRETARY OF THE PREVIOUS ADMINISTRATION, ALEXANDER HAMILTON. BURR BELIEVED HAMILTON HAD HELPED SWING THE PRESIDENCY IN JEFFERSON'S FAVOR AFTER BURR AND JEFFERSON TIED IN THE ELECTORAL VOTE IN 1800. LATER, BURR LOST A RACE FOR THE U.S. SENATE IN NEW YORK STATE. HE AGAIN BLAMED HAMILTON FOR WORKING AGAINST HIM. HE CHALLENGED HAMILTON TO A DUEL AND SHOT HAMILTON TO DEATH ON JULY 11, 1804.

of state. This person sits on the president's right in cabinet meetings and is the voice of the U.S. in foreign affairs. He or she meets with the highest officials of other nations, often negotiating international peace agreements. Five secretaries of state have won the Nobel Peace Prize. Six (Thomas Jefferson, James Madison, James Monroe, John Quincy Adams, Martin Van Buren, and James Buchanan) were elected president. That represents the most from any cabinet position.

The attorney general is the nation's chief law enforcement officer. He or she provides legal advice to the president and top officials. The attorney general also runs the Department of Justice, which is like the world's largest law office.

The Department of the Interior handles issues of land and resources within the

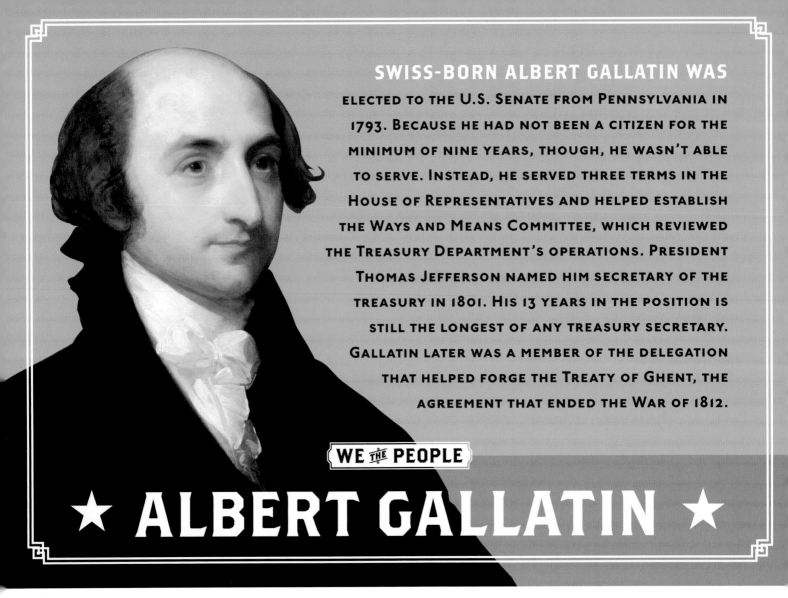

SWISS-BORN ALBERT GALLATIN WAS ELECTED TO THE U.S. SENATE FROM PENNSYLVANIA IN 1793. BECAUSE HE HAD NOT BEEN A CITIZEN FOR THE MINIMUM OF NINE YEARS, THOUGH, HE WASN'T ABLE TO SERVE. INSTEAD, HE SERVED THREE TERMS IN THE HOUSE OF REPRESENTATIVES AND HELPED ESTABLISH THE WAYS AND MEANS COMMITTEE, WHICH REVIEWED THE TREASURY DEPARTMENT'S OPERATIONS. PRESIDENT THOMAS JEFFERSON NAMED HIM SECRETARY OF THE TREASURY IN 1801. HIS 13 YEARS IN THE POSITION IS STILL THE LONGEST OF ANY TREASURY SECRETARY. GALLATIN LATER WAS A MEMBER OF THE DELEGATION THAT HELPED FORGE THE TREATY OF GHENT, THE AGREEMENT THAT ENDED THE WAR OF 1812.

WE THE PEOPLE

★ ALBERT GALLATIN ★

country's borders. Established in 1849, it was the first cabinet position to be added in 60 years. It was formed to respond to the demands of an expanding nation.

From 1861 to 1865, two presidential cabinets existed in North America. One belonged to the U.S. and the other to the Confederate States of America (CSA). CSA president Jefferson Davis's cabinet consisted of the secretaries of four departments—state, treasury, the navy, and war—in addition to a postmaster general and an attorney general. In the 4 years of the CSA's existence, 16 different people served in the 6 cabinet posts, including 6 as secretary of war alone. One of those war secretaries, Judah P. Benjamin, served as both secretary of state and attorney general.

Although most Americans were farmers in the nation's early years, there was

no secretary of agriculture until 1889. From the beginning, the Department of Agriculture has dealt with research and development of seeds, crops, and trees. It has also handled rural issues, food inspection, and nutrition.

A secretary of commerce and **labor** was added to the cabinet in 1903. The aim of the Commerce and Labor Department was, in the words of Missouri congressman Charles F. Cochran, "the conquest of the markets of the world by American merchants and manufacturers." But labor leaders did not want business and labor interests to be represented by the same department. President William Howard

> Most early Americans were farmers, including George Washington (above).

> ★ Its purpose ... was to "promote and develop the welfare of the wage earners of the United States, to improve their working conditions, and to advance their opportunities for profitable employment." ★

NOT IN THE INSTRUCTIONS

Taft authorized a separate Department of Labor on his final day in office in 1913. Its purpose, according to the law that established it, was to "promote and develop the welfare of the wage earners of the United States, to improve their working conditions, and to advance their opportunities for profitable employment."

In 1953, the Department of Health, Education, and Welfare (HEW) was formed. With its broad responsibilities, HEW soon became too costly and difficult to manage. Its budget in 1973 was greater than the DOD's. In 1979, HEW was split into the Department of Education and the Department of Health and Human Services (HHS). The HHS secretary oversees some of the nation's major assistance programs, including Social Security, the Food and Drug Administration, Medicare, Medicaid, and Head Start.

The cabinet added three more departments between 1965 and 1980. The Department of Housing and Urban Development (HUD) was authorized in 1965 to address federal housing policies that would enable more people to own and rent homes. HUD became heavily involved in enforcing lending practices that didn't **discriminate** by race or other factors. Later efforts focused on attracting businesses to struggling cities and towns.

Although a transportation department popped up in several agencies after the Civil War, a secretary of transportation was not part of the president's cabinet until 1966. Since then, the Department of

> The Triangle Shirtwaist Factory fire in New York City on March 25, 1911, killed many and helped spur improved working conditions.

The World.

"Circulation Books Open to All"   "Circulation Books Open to All"

VOL. LI. NO. 18,114   NEW YORK, SUNDAY, MARCH 26, 1911   56 PAGES   PRICE FIVE CENTS.

154 KILLED IN SKYSCRAPER FACTORY FIRE; SCORES BURN, OTHERS LEAP TO DEATH.

BUILDING WHERE FIRE OCCURRED WINDOWS FROM WHICH VICTIMS JUMPED ENCLOSED IN WHITE LINE OF PHOTOGRAPH

GREEN STREET STREWN WITH BODIES

TAGGING VICTIMS FOR IDENTIFICATION.

700 WORKERS, MOSTLY GIRLS, TRAPPED; BODIES OF DEAD HEAP THE STREETS; ONLY ONE FIRE ESCAPE FOR ALL.

Employees Caught on Eighth, Ninth and Tenth Floors—The Blaze Spreads with Great Rapidity—Victims Jump from Window Ledges with Clothing Aflame and Pile Up Below, Dead and Dying—Life Nets Either Torn from Grasp of Rescuers or Burst by Force of Numbers—Criminal Negligence May Be Charged for Locked Fireproof Doors Leading to Stairs—Blaze Is in Triangle Waist Co. Rooms, Washington Place and Greene St.

At 4.35 o'clock yesterday afternoon fire springing from a source that may never be positively identified was discovered in the rear of the eighth floor of the ten-story building at the northwest corner of Washington place and Greene street, the first of three floors occupied as a factory of the Triangle Waist Company.

At 11.30 o'clock Chief Croker made this statement:

"Every body has been removed. The number taken out, which includes those who jumped from the windows, is 141. The number of those that have died so far in the hospitals is seven, which makes the total number of deaths at this time 148."

At 2 o'clock this morning Chief Croker estimated the total dead as one hundred and fifty-four. He said further: "I expected something of this kind to happen in these so-called fire-proof buildings, which are without adequate protection as far as fire-escapes are concerned."

More than a third of those who lost their lives did so in jumping from windows. The firemen who answered the first of the four alarms turned in found 30 bodies on the pavements of Washington place and Greene street. Almost all of these were girls, as were the great majority of them all.

A single fire escape, a single stairway, one working passenger elevator and one working freight elevator offered the only means of escape from the building. A loft building under the specifications of the law, no other ways of egress were required, and to this fact, which also permitted the use of the building as a factory,

the dreadful toll may be traced. Two other elevators were there, but were not in operation.

The property damage resulting from the fire did not exceed $100,000.

To accommodate the unprecedented number of bodies, the Charities pier at the foot of East Twenty-sixth street was opened, for the first time since the Slocum disaster, with which this will rank, for no fire in a building in New York ever claimed so many lives before.

Inspection by Acting Superintendent of Buildings Ludwig will be made the basis for charges of criminal negligence on the ground that the fire-proof doors leading to one of the inclosed tower stairways were locked.

The list of dead and injured will be found on page 4.

Streets Littered with Bodies of Men and Women.

It was the most appalling horror since the Slocum disaster and the Iroquois Theatre fire in Chicago. Every available ambulance in Manhattan was called upon to cart the dead to the Morgue—bodies charred to unrecognizable blackness or reddened to a sickly hue—as was to be seen by shoulders or limbs protruding through flame-eaten clothing. Men and women, boys and girls were of the dead that littered the street, that is actually the condition—the streets were littered.

The fire began in the eighth story. The flames licked and shot their way up through the other two stories. All three floors were occupied by the Triangle Waist Company. The estimate of the number of the employees at work is put at about 1,000. The proprietors of the concern put the number and give them at this point.

[illegible] for bodies, they had no chance of escape. Before [illegible]

first signs that persons in the street knew that these three top stories had turned into red furnaces in which human creatures were being caught and incinerated was when streaming men and women and boys and girls crowded out on the many window ledges and threw themselves into the streets far below.

They jumped with their clothing ablaze. The hair of some of the girls streamed up in flame as they leaped. Thud after thud sounded on the pavements. It is the ghastly fact that on both the Greene street and the Washington place sides of the building there grew mounds of the dead and dying.

And the worst horror of all was that in this heap of the dead now and then there stirred a limb or sounded a moan.

Skeletons Bending Over the Machines.

Within the three flaming floors it was as frightful. There flame enveloped many so that they died instantly. When Fire Chief Croker could make his way into these three floors he found sights that utterly staggered him—that sent him, a man used to viewing horrors, back and down into the street with quivering lips.

The floors were black with smoke. And then he saw as the smoke

drifted away bodies burned to bare bones. There were skeletons bending over sewing machines.

Heroic Elevator Boys Saved Hundreds.

The elevator boys saved hundreds. They each made twenty trips from the time of the alarm until twenty minutes later when they could do no more. Fire was streaming into the shaft, flames biting at the cables. They died for their own lives.

Some—about seventy—chose a successful avenue of escape. They clambered up a ladder to the roof. A few remembered the fire escape. Many never thought of it, but only as they entered ribs of dismay.

[illegible] [illegible] this fire escape—a loose ladder running [illegible] and narrow reach which was never filled as the fire raged, one [illegible] slowly greeted second to the ladder. If, the scene they fought and struggled and breathed free, and died trying to squeeze that needle-eye road to self-preservation.

Those who got the roof—got life. Young men of the University of New York Commercial and Law School, studious young fellows who had chosen to spend their Saturday afternoon in study, answered the yells for aid that came from the smoking roof by thrusting ladders from the

THE EXECUTIVE DEPARTMENTS

DEPARTMENT OF STATE

DEPARTMENT OF THE TREASURY

DEPARTMENT OF DEFENSE

DEPARTMENT OF JUSTICE

DEPARTMENT OF THE INTERIOR

DEPARTMENT OF AGRICULTURE

DEPARTMENT OF COMMERCE

DEPARTMENT OF LABOR

DEPARTMENT OF HEALTH AND HUMAN SERVICES

DEPARTMENT OF HOUSING AND URBAN DEVELOPMENT

DEPARTMENT OF TRANSPORTATION

DEPARTMENT OF ENERGY

DEPARTMENT OF EDUCATION

DEPARTMENT OF VETERANS AFFAIRS

DEPARTMENT OF HOMELAND SECURITY

RONALD REAGAN

Transportation (DOT) has become instrumental in establishing design and safety standards for motor vehicles and highways. It also governs and coordinates transportation on railroads, in the air, and on some of the nation's waterways.

When oil-producing countries in the Middle East stopped sending oil to the U.S. in 1973, the price of gasoline skyrocketed. There was barely enough oil to go around. People started to worry about U.S. dependence on foreign oil. It led to the creation of the Department of Energy (DOE) under president Jimmy Carter in 1977.

As American involvement in major warfare increased throughout the 19th and 20th centuries, so did the number of military veterans. These people often needed healthcare, education, job training, and other assistance. Scattered agencies were brought together into the cabinet as the Department of Veterans Affairs in 1989. The law enabling that organization was signed in 1988 by president Ronald Reagan.

The 15th cabinet position, the secretary of homeland security, was first filled in 2003. In the aftermath of the September 11, 2001, terror attacks, president George W. Bush formed the Office of Homeland Security. The following year, it became a department (DHS). It combined long-standing agencies such as the Coast Guard, Border Patrol, and Immigration and Naturalization Service into one.

> The number of cabinet departments has been stabilized at 15 since Homeland Security was added in 2002.

STEVEN CHU
★ Secretary of Energy ★
January 21, 2009 – April 22, 2013

WILLIAM H. SEWARD
★ Secretary of State ★
March 6, 1861 – March 4, 1869

ALEXANDER HAMILTON
Secretary of the Treasury ★ September 11, 1789 – January 31, 1795

SALMON P. CHASE
★ Secretary of the Treasury ★
March 7, 1861 – June 30, 1864

ELIHU ROOT
★ Secretary of War ★
August 1, 1899 – January 31, 1904
★ Secretary of State ★
July 19, 1905 – January 27, 1909

CORDELL HULL
★ Secretary of State ★
March 4, 1933 – November 30, 1944

GEORGE MARSHALL
★ Secretary of State ★
January 21, 1947 – January 20, 1949
★ Secretary of Defense ★
September 21, 1950 – September 12, 1951

FRANK B. KELLOGG
Secretary of State ★ March 5, 1925 – March 28, 1929

JOHN QUINCY ADAMS
Secretary of State ★ September 22, 1817 – March 3, 1825
President of the United States ★ March 4, 1825 – March 4, 1829

HENRY KISSINGER
★ Secretary of State ★
September 22, 1973 – January 20, 1977

SUPERSTAR SECRETARIES

THE PRESIDENTIAL CABINET

A president chooses cabinet members based on their area of experience. A secretary of labor, for example, would be expected to know about workplaces, management, and economics. Those who helped the president get elected are also often given cabinet posts. But it's not all about politics. Many cabinet members come from colleges and universities, where they are top scholars in their field. Energy secretary Steven Chu was appointed during president Barack Obama's first term. He won the Nobel Prize in Physics in 1997 and was a professor of physics and biology at the University of California, Berkeley. Henry Kissinger, secretary of state under both Richard Nixon and Gerald Ford, had a doctorate in political science from Harvard. He taught there before entering the cabinet, where he won a Nobel Peace Prize.

★ **They've influenced economics, relationships with other nations, and even the very shape of the nation itself.** ★

SUPERSTAR SECRETARIES

Cabinet officials are called "secretaries" for several reasons. The root of the word ("secret") suggests that a cabinet official is someone who can guard sensitive information. But in many countries, the term "minister" is used instead for the same position. "Minister" carries a religious meaning that the Founders did not want in the U.S. government. They tried to separate church and state.

Cabinet members tend to serve short terms. Of those appointed by two-term presidents, few serve the full eight years. There are several reasons for that. First, they're not elected, so they don't have a set term. Second, the jobs are pressure-packed, and the people who hold them are often presented with many opportunities for advancement elsewhere. Third, they serve until the president just doesn't like their advice. Then they resign, which can be either their idea or the president's. The exception to all this was secretary of agriculture James Wilson. He served four presidents from 1897 to 1913. It was the longest anyone has ever held a cabinet post.

Although some cabinet members have gone on to become president, others who have served only as department heads still made names for themselves in U.S. history. They've influenced economics, relationships with other nations, and even the very shape of the nation itself.

Alexander Hamilton may be the best example of a cabinet secretary whose views

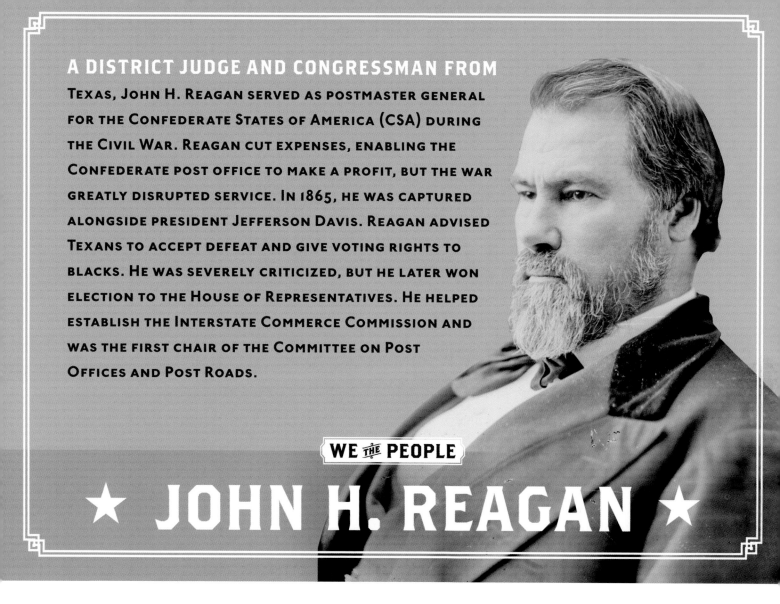

★ JOHN H. REAGAN ★

A DISTRICT JUDGE AND CONGRESSMAN FROM TEXAS, JOHN H. REAGAN SERVED AS POSTMASTER GENERAL FOR THE CONFEDERATE STATES OF AMERICA (CSA) DURING THE CIVIL WAR. REAGAN CUT EXPENSES, ENABLING THE CONFEDERATE POST OFFICE TO MAKE A PROFIT, BUT THE WAR GREATLY DISRUPTED SERVICE. IN 1865, HE WAS CAPTURED ALONGSIDE PRESIDENT JEFFERSON DAVIS. REAGAN ADVISED TEXANS TO ACCEPT DEFEAT AND GIVE VOTING RIGHTS TO BLACKS. HE WAS SEVERELY CRITICIZED, BUT HE LATER WON ELECTION TO THE HOUSE OF REPRESENTATIVES. HE HELPED ESTABLISH THE INTERSTATE COMMERCE COMMISSION AND WAS THE FIRST CHAIR OF THE COMMITTEE ON POST OFFICES AND POST ROADS.

and policies had a lasting effect on the nation. Hamilton, a close aide to Washington during the Revolutionary War, was the first treasury secretary. He established **tariffs**, which enabled the federal government to pay off $15 million in debts from the war. Modern Americans probably recognize him because his face is on the $10 bill. But Hamilton also thought deeply and wrote extensively about the nature of government.

He wanted the central (federal) government to be more powerful than the state governments. Hamilton believed the president's powers should take authority in many matters over the states. That view put him at odds with Thomas Jefferson, the first secretary of state and the third president. He thought a strong president was too much like a king. Still, many historians say the U.S. has developed to resemble Hamilton's

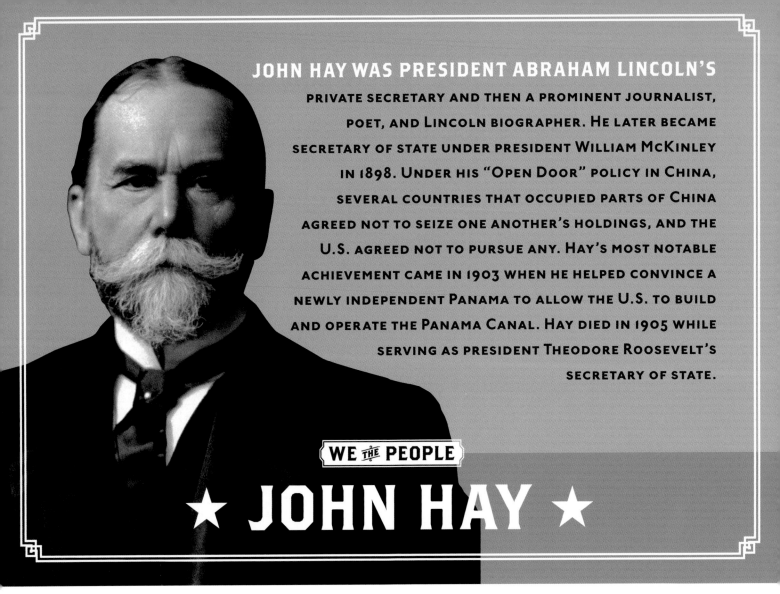

JOHN HAY WAS PRESIDENT ABRAHAM LINCOLN'S PRIVATE SECRETARY AND THEN A PROMINENT JOURNALIST, POET, AND LINCOLN BIOGRAPHER. HE LATER BECAME SECRETARY OF STATE UNDER PRESIDENT WILLIAM MCKINLEY IN 1898. UNDER HIS "OPEN DOOR" POLICY IN CHINA, SEVERAL COUNTRIES THAT OCCUPIED PARTS OF CHINA AGREED NOT TO SEIZE ONE ANOTHER'S HOLDINGS, AND THE U.S. AGREED NOT TO PURSUE ANY. HAY'S MOST NOTABLE ACHIEVEMENT CAME IN 1903 WHEN HE HELPED CONVINCE A NEWLY INDEPENDENT PANAMA TO ALLOW THE U.S. TO BUILD AND OPERATE THE PANAMA CANAL. HAY DIED IN 1905 WHILE SERVING AS PRESIDENT THEODORE ROOSEVELT'S SECRETARY OF STATE.

★ JOHN HAY ★

overall vision for the nation.

Salmon P. Chase was another influential treasury secretary. Serving under Lincoln during the Civil War, he established the national banking system. Chase also introduced paper currency, putting his own face on the first $1 bill in 1862. From 1918 to 1946, Chase's image was printed on the $10,000 bill in honor of his place in history.

Some historians consider John Quincy Adams the most distinguished secretary of state. By the time he was in his early 30s, Adams had served as U.S. minister to the Netherlands, Portugal, and Prussia. After a stint in the U.S. Senate, he accepted further diplomatic appointments in Russia and Great Britain. He helped negotiate the treaty that ended the War of 1812. Named secretary of state by president James Monroe, Adams made a deal with Spain to

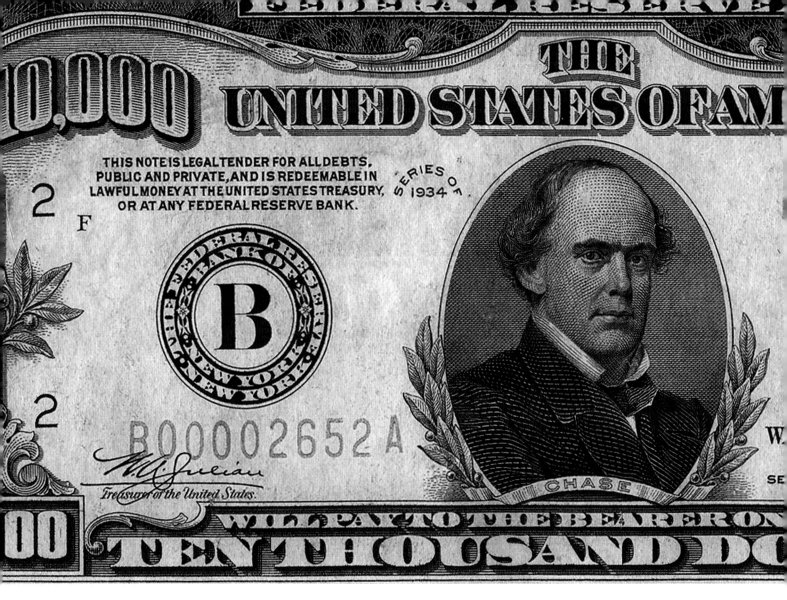

acquire Florida and settled boundary arguments with Britain. Adams also helped Monroe declare an end to European colonization in the Americas. Adams later served one term as president. Following that, he represented Massachusetts for 17 years in the U.S. House. This made him one of only two former presidents to ever serve in the legislative branch after their time as chief executive. As a representative, he also argued before the U.S. Supreme Court that 53 Africans who had **mutinied** on a slave ship en route to Cuba should be returned to Africa. That trial became the subject of the 1997 Hollywood film, *Amistad*.

> After his term as treasury secretary, Chase sat on the Supreme Court bench.

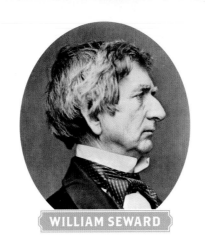

★ These actions amplified American influence across the Western Hemisphere. ★

SUPERSTAR SECRETARIES

Lincoln's secretary of state, William Seward, was considered to be more powerful than the president. That's one reason he was stabbed the same night Lincoln was assassinated. Four supporters of the Confederacy had plotted to kill Lincoln, Seward, and vice president Andrew Johnson to bring down the Union government. Seward survived and continued in his post as secretary of state under Johnson. He negotiated the purchases of Alaska and Midway Island. He also laid the groundwork for the purchase of the Panama Canal zone. These actions amplified American influence across the Western Hemisphere.

When Seward signed a treaty with Russia to purchase Alaska for $7.2 million in 1867, the deal was known as "Seward's Folly."

George Marshall illustrated how a secretary of state could fashion a positive international image for the country. Marshall earned fame as U.S. Army Chief of Staff during World War II and was appointed secretary of state in 1947. He helped draft a proposal that became known as the Marshall Plan, a $13-billion initiative to rebuild western Europe after the war. Marshall resigned from the State Department in 1949. However, president Harry Truman called him back as

MAP OF
ALASKA

SCALES.

Statute Miles, 69.16=

Kilometres, 111.307=

ORDER of ESTABLISHMENT OF EXECUTIVE DEPARTMENTS

1789   DEPARTMENT OF STATE
DEPARTMENT OF THE TREASURY
DEPARTMENT OF WAR
DEPARTMENT OF THE NAVY

1849   DEPARTMENT OF THE INTERIOR

1862   DEPARTMENT OF AGRICULTURE

1870   DEPARTMENT OF JUSTICE

1903   DEPARTMENT OF COMMERCE AND LABOR

1913   DEPARTMENT OF COMMERCE AND LABOR SPLITS TO FORM **DEPARTMENT OF COMMERCE** AND **DEPARTMENT OF LABOR**

1949   DEPARTMENT OF NAVY AND DEPARTMENT OF WAR MERGE TO FORM THE DEPARTMENT OF DEFENSE

1953   DEPARTMENT OF HEALTH, EDUCATION, AND WELFARE

1965   DEPARTMENT OF HOUSING AND URBAN DEVELOPMENT

1966   DEPARTMENT OF TRANSPORTATION

1977   DEPARTMENT OF ENERGY

1979   DEPARTMENT OF HEALTH, EDUCATION, AND WELFARE SPLITS TO FORM DEPARTMENT OF EDUCATION AND DEPARTMENT OF HEALTH AND HUMAN SERVICES

1989   DEPARTMENT OF VETERANS AFFAIRS

2002   DEPARTMENT OF HOMELAND SECURITY

5

CABINET SECRETARIES HAVE WON THE

NOBEL PEACE PRIZE

ELIHU ROOT
FRANK B. KELLOGG
CORDELL HULL
GEORGE MARSHALL
HENRY KISSINGER

16

YEARS SERVED

BY LONGEST-SERVING CABINET MEMBER
JAMES WILSON
SECRETARY OF AGRICULTURE
1897-1913

2

INCHES

THE PRESIDENT'S CHAIR IS TWO INCHES TALLER THAN THE CABINET MEMBERS' CHAIRS IN THE WHITE HOUSE'S CABINET ROOM.

SUPERSTAR SECRETARIES

secretary of defense in 1950 during the Korean War. After only a year in that post, Marshall retired from office for good.

In 1953, Marshall became the fourth secretary of state to win the Nobel Peace Prize. Elihu Root, who under Theodore Roosevelt crafted numerous peace treaties and established international courts, was the first, in 1913. Frank B. Kellogg, whose name is on an international agreement reached after World War I that attempted to avoid further wars, won the 1929 award. And Cordell Hull, Franklin D. Roosevelt's secretary of state, a designer of the United Nations, was recognized for that effort in 1945. After Marshall,

Secretary Kissinger was the fifth to receive the Peace Prize. In 1973, he and Le Duc Tho of North Vietnam were supposed to share it for the ceasefire agreement that brought the Vietnam War to a close.

Secretaries of other departments have also made their mark on U.S. and world history. Before he became president of the CSA, Jefferson Davis, for example, was secretary of war under president Franklin Pierce from 1853 to 1857. President Lincoln's eldest son, Robert Todd Lincoln, was also secretary of war. He served from 1881 to 1885 under presidents James Garfield and Chester A. Arthur.

> Commissioned as a second lieutenant in 1902, Marshall ended his army career in 1959 as a five-star general.

THE ORIGINAL KITCHEN CABINET

FRANCIS PRESTON BLAIR

MARTIN VAN BUREN

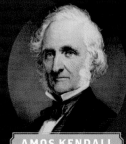

AMOS KENDALL

ROGER B. TANEY

PRESIDENT ANDREW JACKSON

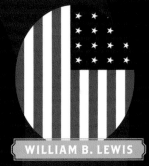

WILLIAM B. LEWIS

ISAAC HILL

ANDREW J. DONELSON

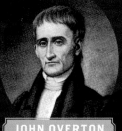

DUFF GREEN

JOHN OVERTON

Jackson's **KITCHEN CABINET** consisted of nine of his longtime political allies.

CHAPTER 3

THE NATURE OF THE JOB

THE PRESIDENTIAL CABINET

President Andrew Jackson found shortly after he became president in 1829 that his strategy for picking cabinet chiefs had backfired. Over time, he came to distrust at least three of them. He thought they were more loyal to vice president John C. Calhoun. So when Jackson needed to discuss important matters without involving Calhoun, he turned to people *outside* the cabinet. These advisers never met in the room where Cabinet meetings were held. People began to joke that Jackson was consulting with his most trusted advisers in the White House kitchen, so the group became known as the Kitchen Cabinet.

Kitchen Cabinets have become more common since Jackson's time. And their members haven't always been secretive or shadowy figures. One of Jackson's key background advisers, Francis

★ **Such presidential confidantes may be viewed with some suspicion, because they are not appointed or voted on by the Senate.** ★

THE NATURE OF THE JOB

Preston Blair, was the publisher of the *Washington Globe*. He would meet with Jackson, and then write about Jackson's ideas in the newspaper. Blair, who also established what became the impartial *Congressional Record*, remained influential in politics for several decades. He served as a Kitchen Cabinet adviser to Lincoln.

Such presidential confidantes may be viewed with some suspicion, because they are not appointed or voted on by the Senate. However, many offer valuable expertise and political insights. First Ladies such as Abigail Adams, Eleanor Roosevelt, Nancy Reagan, and, of course, Hillary Clinton (who later became secretary of state) have played such a role as well. Edith Wilson, the second wife of president Woodrow Wilson, came out of the wings after the president suffered a stroke in 1919. She limited everyday communications and public contact for the partially paralyzed president for the rest of his term.

But under President Nixon, personal advisers came to illustrate how high-level secrecy can corrupt government. John Ehrlichman, Nixon's chief domestic adviser, and H. R. Haldeman, the White House chief of staff, were convicted of major crimes for their roles in the **Watergate scandal** that forced Nixon to resign the presidency. Also convicted was attorney general John Mitchell, who of course had been in Nixon's cabinet.

FRANCES PERKINS WAS THE FIRST WOMAN TO SERVE IN THE PRESIDENTIAL CABINET. BUT SHE WAS AN OBVIOUS CHOICE FOR PRESIDENT FRANKLIN D. ROOSEVELT WHEN HE NAMED HER SECRETARY OF LABOR IN 1933. PERKINS HAD BEEN LABOR COMMISSIONER IN NEW YORK STATE WHEN ROOSEVELT WAS GOVERNOR. AS U.S. LABOR SECRETARY, SHE WORKED FOR MINIMUM WAGE LAWS AND ON VARIOUS PARTS OF ROOSEVELT'S EMPLOYMENT AND RELIEF PROGRAMS DURING THE GREAT DEPRESSION. PERKINS HELPED ESTABLISH UNEMPLOYMENT BENEFITS UNDER THE SOCIAL SECURITY PROGRAM. SHE WAS 1 OF ONLY 2 PEOPLE TO SERVE IN ROOSEVELT'S CABINET FOR HIS ENTIRE 12-YEAR PRESIDENCY, BECOMING THE LONGEST-SERVING LABOR SECRETARY.

WE THE PEOPLE

★ FRANCES PERKINS ★

When not involved in intrigue and drama, cabinets also have a routine nature. Under some presidents, the cabinets have met every week. Reagan met with his twice a week. President Obama held cabinet meetings about every two months. "A lot of them are doing such good jobs that they don't meet with me much," Obama said. "They're like the good students in class. They're just handling their business really well." Still, Obama said, it's important that the department secretaries "know they have my ear," and that they get together to maintain a sense of **camaraderie**. Gary Locke, Obama's secretary of commerce from March 2009 to August 2011, remarked that cabinet meetings are "an incredible way for everyone to communicate, for everyone to really understand what the issues are, and to help us all get on the same

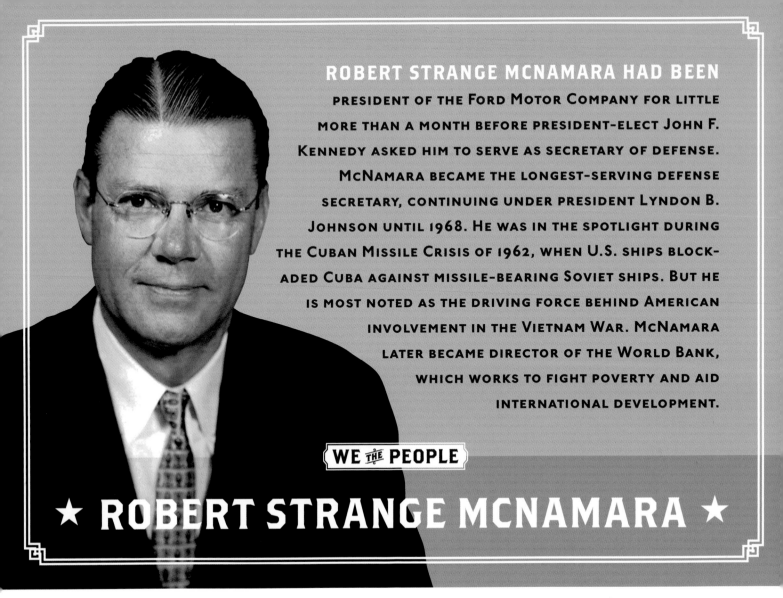

ROBERT STRANGE MCNAMARA HAD BEEN PRESIDENT OF THE FORD MOTOR COMPANY FOR LITTLE MORE THAN A MONTH BEFORE PRESIDENT-ELECT JOHN F. KENNEDY ASKED HIM TO SERVE AS SECRETARY OF DEFENSE. MCNAMARA BECAME THE LONGEST-SERVING DEFENSE SECRETARY, CONTINUING UNDER PRESIDENT LYNDON B. JOHNSON UNTIL 1968. HE WAS IN THE SPOTLIGHT DURING THE CUBAN MISSILE CRISIS OF 1962, WHEN U.S. SHIPS BLOCKADED CUBA AGAINST MISSILE-BEARING SOVIET SHIPS. BUT HE IS MOST NOTED AS THE DRIVING FORCE BEHIND AMERICAN INVOLVEMENT IN THE VIETNAM WAR. MCNAMARA LATER BECAME DIRECTOR OF THE WORLD BANK, WHICH WORKS TO FIGHT POVERTY AND AID INTERNATIONAL DEVELOPMENT.

WE THE PEOPLE

★ ROBERT STRANGE MCNAMARA ★

page so that we can advance the President's priorities."

Cabinet meetings are the only occasions that find all members in one room. Even for the annual State of the Union address, for example, one cabinet member is asked not to attend. In theory, that's because if there were some disaster or attack, at least one presidential successor would still be alive. Cabinet meetings are held in a room next to

the Oval Office. Members gather around an elliptical table purchased by Nixon in 1970. The president sits in the middle on one of the long sides of the table. His chair is two inches (5 cm) taller than those of the secretaries. The vice president sits opposite the president. On the president's right is the secretary of state, and the treasury secretary is to the right of the vice president. The secretary of defense sits on the left side of

the president. To the vice president's left is the attorney general. The other secretaries are arranged according to when their departments were added to the cabinet.

Joining this group are seven other key advisers who are members of the cabinet but are not department secretaries. They are the White House chief of staff, the administrator of the Environmental Protection Agency, the director of the Office of Management and Budget, the U.S. Trade Representative, the American ambassador to the United Nations, the chairman of the Council of Economic Advisers, and the administrator of the Small Business Administration.

> **Lincoln famously (and unusually) chose his political rivals to serve in the cabinet.**

THE NATURE OF THE JOB

Cabinet secretaries' responsibilities would seem to be as clear as the names of their departments. But those responsibilities often change, expand, and overlap—sometimes in strange ways. In the 1930s, for example, the Department of Agriculture got involved in bringing electricity to rural homes. It also began providing **subsidies** to farmers to protect them from wild swings in crop prices. Today, the department is deeply interested in alternative-energy issues. Wherever crops, waste, or other such resources could be seen as possible sources of energy, Agriculture wants to know. It's also involved because wind energy is often generated from **turbines** that stand in fields where only crops used to grow.

Following the Civil War, the Treasury Department led the fight against one of the chief economic threats of the day, the **counterfeiting** of U.S. currency. In response, the Secret Service was formed and became part of Treasury. The Secret Service is still involved in tracking down counterfeiters, but its far more well-known task is protecting the president. The agency shifted to DHS in 2003.

In 1919, the states authorized a constitutional **amendment** that prohibited the sale, manufacture, storage, and transportation of alcoholic beverages in the U.S. This was known as Prohibition. From 1920 to 1930, enforcement was the job of the Treasury Department, since violations were regarded as failures to pay taxes. Between 1930 and 1933, enforcement switched to the Department of Justice, and

> The entire 18th Amendment on prohibition was eventually repealed, or overturned, in 1933 by the 21st Amendment.

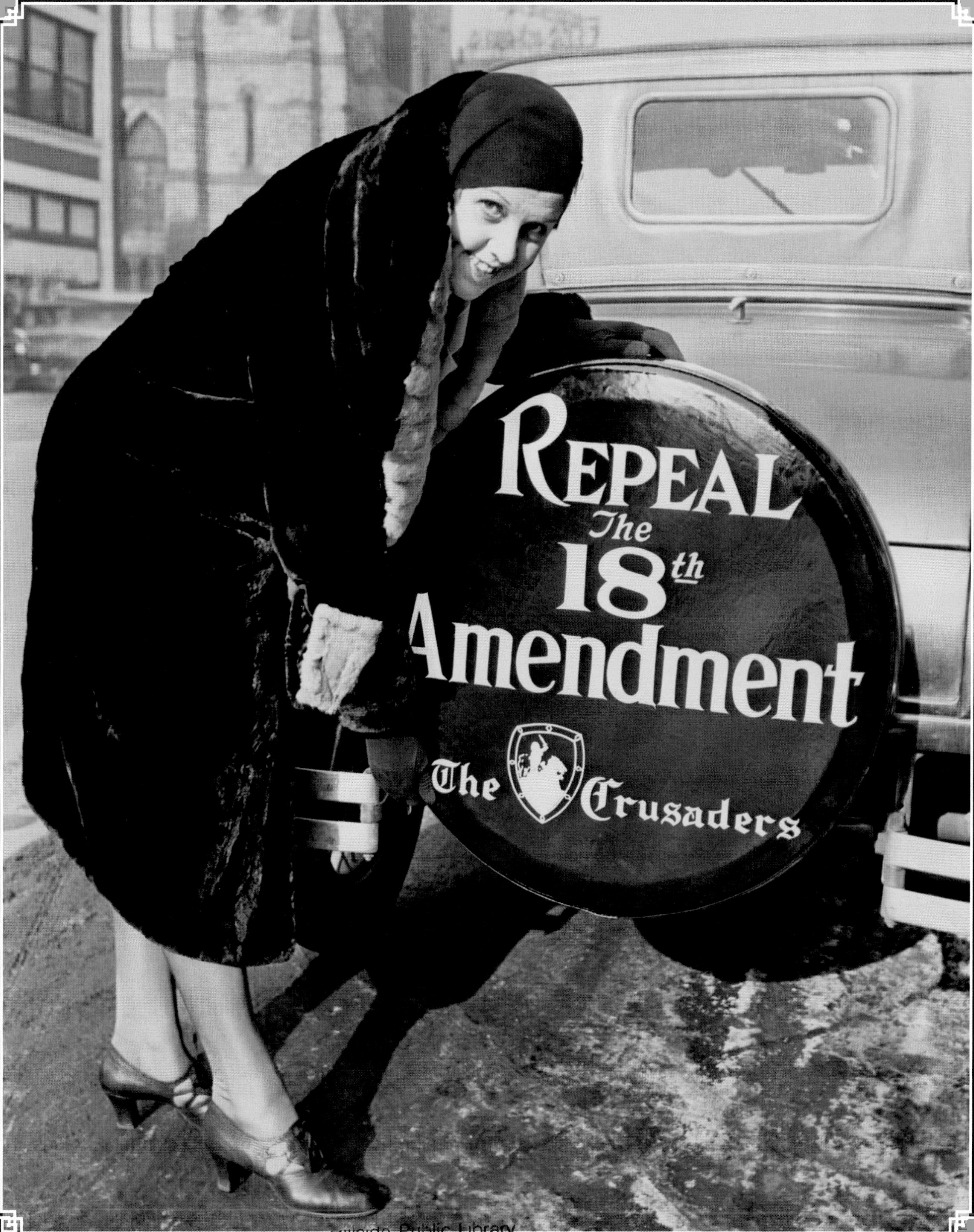
REPEAL
The
18th
Amendment
The Crusaders

DEPARTMENT OF THE INTERIOR

BUREAU OF INDIAN AFFAIRS

BUREAU OF LAND MANAGEMENT

BUREAU OF OCEAN ENERGY MANAGEMENT

BUREAU OF RECLAMATION

BUREAU OF SAFETY AND ENVIRONMENT ENFORCEMENT

NATIONAL PARK SERVICE

OFFICE OF INSULAR AFFAIRS

OFFICE OF SURFACE MINING, RECLAMATION, AND ENFORCEMENT

U.S. FISH AND WILDLIFE SERVICE

U.S. GEOLOGICAL SURVEY

According to a 2010 DOI report, energy projects on federally managed lands and offshore areas supply about 30 percent of the nation's energy production. This includes:

☛ **17%** of hydropower

☛ **35%** of oil

☛ **39%** of natural gas

☛ **42%** of coal

☛ **50%** of geothermal

DOI manages **184** Indian schools serving **47,671** students.

DOI manages **507** million acres of surface land, or about one-fifth of the land in the U.S. (represented in red above).

GRAND CANYON

then the Federal Bureau of Investigation (FBI). When alcohol once again became an openly sold and taxable commodity in 1933, its control and oversight returned to the Treasury Department.

When the Department of Commerce and Labor was formed in 1903, it unsurprisingly promoted mining, manufacturing, shipping, fishing, and labor interests. But it was also put in charge of immigration, perhaps because of all the potential workers entering the country. Today, immigration issues are the domain of DHS instead. Commerce continues to keep an eye on business and trade, but it's also responsible for the National

Oceanic and Atmospheric Administration (NOAA), which includes the National Weather Service. It supervises the Census Bureau and the **Patent** Office, too.

The Department of the Interior, meanwhile, may be a bigger part of Americans' lives than they realize. While it manages the Bureau of Land Management and the Bureau of Indian Affairs, it also includes the National Park Service, the U.S. Fish and Wildlife Service, and the U.S. Geological Survey (USGS). The USGS produces **topographic** maps popular with hikers, campers, and other outdoorspeople.

> The "interior" part of DOI's name has to do with the interior of the nation—the department manages areas *inside* the U.S.

TWO CONTROVERSIAL PROGRAMS

NO CHILD LEFT BEHIND

SIGNED INTO LAW BY

PRESIDENT GEORGE W. BUSH

ON JANUARY 8, 2002

DEPARTMENT OF EDUCATION

WHAT IS IT? NCLB requires all public schools receiving federal funding to administer a statewide standardized test every year.

WHY CONTROVERSIAL? Some think it: gives too much control of eduction to the federal government ★ forces teachers to "teach to the test" ★ places too much strain on schools to meet "adequate yearly progress" benchmarks ★ is not adequately funded

AFFORDABLE CARE ACT

SIGNED INTO LAW BY

PRESIDENT BARACK OBAMA

ON MARCH 23, 2010

DEPARTMENT OF HEALTH
AND HUMAN SERVICES

WHAT IS IT? The ACA was enacted to increase the quality and affordability of health insurance, lower the uninsured rate by expanding public and private insurance coverage, and reduce the costs of healthcare for individuals and the government.

WHY CONTROVERSIAL? Some think it: goes beyond the federal government's scope ★ restricts health insurance companies ★ is unfair to require every individual to have health insurance

CHAPTER № 4

CHANGING CHALLENGES

THE PRESIDENTIAL CABINET

From an original cabinet of 4 departments to today's group of 15, the scope of the cabinet has reflected the ever-increasing complexity of the country. Departments have always been the largest building blocks of the federal government. They're where the everyday work of government gets done—where licenses get issued, where papers get signed, and where money gets distributed. But cabinet departments and their hundreds of sub-agencies are also where a president's policies get put into action. And those moves can be intensely controversial. Today, they might involve how cars get designed, what kids get for lunch at school, whether a new highway gets constructed, or if a housing complex gets built in your neighborhood.

★ Secretaries and agency heads can also come to symbolize all the negative feelings people might have about a president. ★

CHANGING CHALLENGES

When a new president gets elected, the rules often change, and it's the cabinet departments and sub-agencies that carry them out. As a result, cabinet departments or the secretaries themselves are often targeted with intense criticism from the public, the news media, and congresspeople. President Obama's Affordable Care Act, for example, was such a far-reaching new program that it put HHS, which administers it, under a spotlight for several years. Cabinet secretaries may also be used as weapons, with the president keeping them in office as a way of standing up to his political opponents and pushing his policies forward. Sometimes they are victims, resigning or getting fired when they bring too much heat

on the president or when they disagree with him. Secretaries and agency heads can also come to symbolize all the negative feelings people might have about a president. This happened with Michael Brown when the Federal Emergency Management Agency (or FEMA, part of DHS since 2003) botched the response to Hurricane Katrina in New Orleans, early in president George W. Bush's second term.

Of all the cabinet departments, the one that seems to be most often under attack is the Department of Education. For much of the nation's history, teachers and what they taught were regulated by local school boards overseen by state agencies. Many citizens and policymakers believe education should

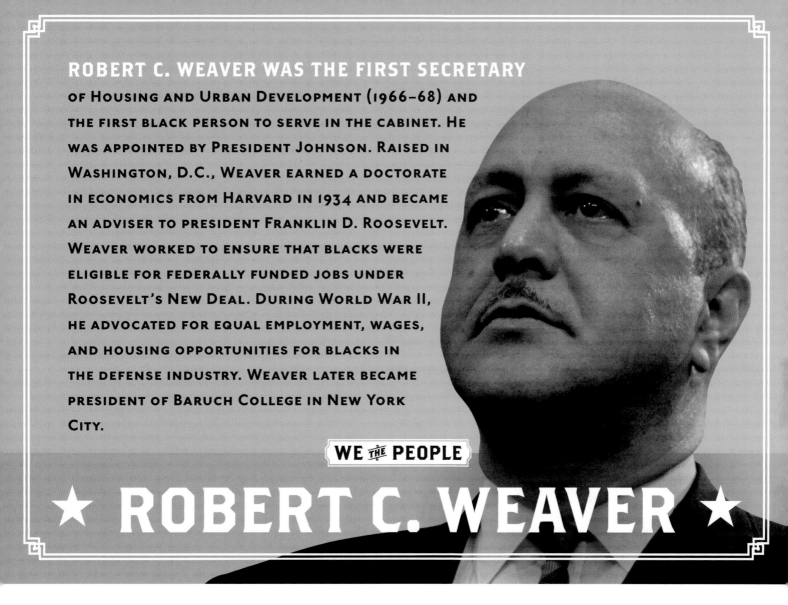

ROBERT C. WEAVER WAS THE FIRST SECRETARY of Housing and Urban Development (1966–68) and the first black person to serve in the cabinet. He was appointed by President Johnson. Raised in Washington, D.C., Weaver earned a doctorate in economics from Harvard in 1934 and became an adviser to president Franklin D. Roosevelt. Weaver worked to ensure that blacks were eligible for federally funded jobs under Roosevelt's New Deal. During World War II, he advocated for equal employment, wages, and housing opportunities for blacks in the defense industry. Weaver later became president of Baruch College in New York City.

WE THE PEOPLE

★ ROBERT C. WEAVER ★

reflect that approach today. The idea of the federal government setting rules for education in all 50 states angers them. That's one reason why, since the day the Department of Education began in 1979, many people have wanted to drop it. Reagan called for its elimination in his State of the Union address only three years later. For much of the past 30 years, Republican presidential candidates have backed proposals to get rid of the Department of Education.

In 2002, Republican president George W. Bush ran counter to that opposition with a program called No Child Left Behind (NCLB). It required all schools that received federal funding to give an annual standardized test. Schools were supposed to show improvement in those test scores every year or they would have to do other things to make progress. The program greatly expanded

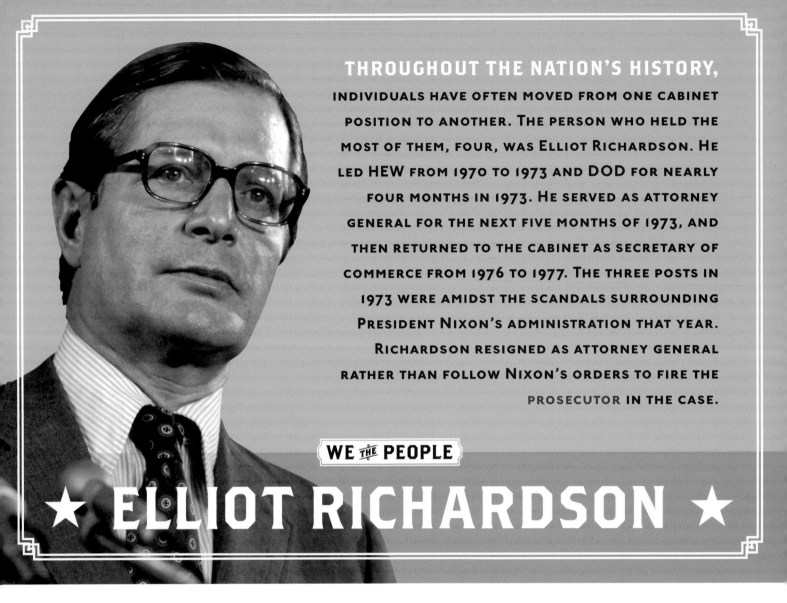

WE THE PEOPLE

★ ELLIOT RICHARDSON ★

the Department of Education's influence, which many resented. The Obama administration continued to field attacks on NCLB and the department. Internet petitions and even bumper stickers sounded the call to have secretary Arne Duncan removed. In 2015, Republican senator Rand Paul sharply referred to the entire department as "an overreach of constitutional authority by the federal government."

That kind of opposition to a cabinet department's activities isn't new. In fact, sometimes it comes from within the department itself or from the groups the department is supposed to be serving. James Watt, interior secretary under President Reagan, alienated many in the **conservation** and environmental communities for his expansion of mining, drilling, and other uses of public land by private industry. Watt served only two years in

the post. In 1995, he was charged with lying about his lobbying work at HUD after he left office. In 2008, *Time* magazine named him one of the worst cabinet members in modern times.

Cabinet departments and their secretaries face a rapidly changing landscape of issues. Their jobs are likely to change dramatically in the future, with some becoming much more visible. The Department of Energy, for example, will likely have to confront issues stemming from the surprising expansion of oil drilling in the U.S. That, and international responses to the drilling, are likely to change the economic and environmental concerns surrounding oil.

> **Balancing public land use with wilderness conservation is a challenge for the cabinet.**

> ★ **Although scientists generally agree on the causes of global warming, politicians do not. As a result, debates about how to deal with it continue to be contentious.** ★

CHANGING CHALLENGES

Conversely, the department is expected to play a big role in the development of renewable energy sources.

The newest cabinet department, Homeland Security, has in less than a decade become familiar to Americans in many ways. Its Transportation Security Administration (TSA) X-rays and inspects people and baggage at airports. Because DHS also supervises immigration, it is becoming a key player in issues of border security and terrorism.

Although scientists generally agree on the causes of global warming, politicians do

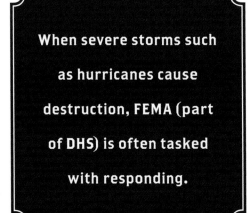

When severe storms such as hurricanes cause destruction, FEMA (part of DHS) is often tasked with responding.

not. As a result, debates about how to deal with it continue to be contentious. And because it will affect various sectors, from food supply to public **infrastructure** to public health, it is likely to embroil secretaries of departments such as Agriculture, Transportation, and perhaps even DHS. A warmer climate is expected to bring more severe storms and floods, and FEMA, which deals with disaster response, is now part of Homeland Security.

In 1989, a new secretary of transportation, Samuel Skinner, indicated his main challenges would be attacking terrorism

CONTROVERSIAL CABINET MEMBERS

ALBERT FALL

SECRETARY OF THE INTERIOR ★ 1921–23

Fall was the first cabinet member to be convicted of a felony. In 1922, he accepted more than $400,000 from oil companies in exchange for the right to drill on federal lands, including the Teapot Dome reserve in Wyoming.

JOHN MITCHELL
★ ATTORNEY GENERAL 1969–72 ★

While in office, Mitchell approved unconstitutional wiretaps, among other questionable acts. In 1975, he was convicted of helping plan and cover up the burglary at the Watergate Hotel.

MICHAEL BROWN
★ DIRECTOR OF FEMA 2003–05 ★

Brown was highly criticized for FEMA's response to Hurricane Katrina, one of the worst natural disasters in U.S. history. He resigned two weeks after the storm struck.

JAMES WATT

SECRETARY OF THE INTERIOR ★ 1981–83

In Watt's two years in office, the leasing of federal lands to mining and drilling companies increased fivefold. In 1996, he pled guilty to withholding evidence from a federal grand jury investigation.

EARL BUTZ

SECRETARY OF AGRICULTURE ★ 1971–76

Butz was apt to spew insulting racist and prejudicial remarks. After a particularly crude joke was widely reported, Butz was pressured to resign. Five years later, in 1981, Butz pled guilty to tax evasion.

HAZEL O'LEARY
★ SECRETARY OF ENERGY 1993–97 ★

An audit of O'Leary's exorbitant travel expenses led to her 1997 resignation. Later that year, the DOJ investigated whether O'Leary agreed to meet with Chinese officials after they made a donation to her favorite charity.

CHANGING CHALLENGES

and drug trafficking. Twenty-five years later, the challenges were still there, but the department handling them was different: DHS. However, at the beginning of 2015, DHS was dealing with another hazard in Congress itself. Caught up in divisions along party lines, Congress threatened to not approve DHS funding. But a last-second agreement was reached in March to pay for some of the agency's activities.

With the attacks of September 11, 2001, large-scale terrorism within the U.S. was no longer a threat but a reality.

Cabinet secretaries are both shielded by and vulnerable to a president's priorities. Their departments are protected by history, size, and how deeply they are woven into the workings of the federal government. But Congress, as well as the very course of national and international events, will continue to affect the president's cabinet—its makeup, its work, and its importance in the everyday life of the American people.

amendment   a change, clarification, or addition to the U.S. Constitution, proposed by Congress and approved by three-fourths of the states

camaraderie   a sense of trust and friendship in a group

conflicts of interest   situations in which a government official has a private activity or relationship that can compromise or generate personal profit from his or her government work

conservation   the preservation and protection of natural resources

counterfeiting   making imitation or fraudulent money

discriminate   to make a distinction in favor of or against a person based on race, gender, religion, or some other category, rather than merit

infrastructure   facilities and systems physically supporting the activities of a community, such as roads, bridges, and utility lines

labor   the workforce of a nation

mutinied   revolted against an established authority, most often as sailors against a ship's commander

patent   the exclusive right given to an inventor to make or sell an invention

presidential succession   the order in which top governmental officials are placed in the event that the president dies while in office, resigns, or is otherwise unable to perform the job

prosecutor   in a legal case, the attorney representing the side that accuses another of illegal actions

subsidies   funds paid by a government to an individual, business, or industry, usually to aid growth or as protection from price swings

tariffs   charges, or a kind of tax, on certain imported and exported goods

topographic   having to do with the features of land, such as hills, woods, and bodies of water

turbines   machines that convert the forces of wind, water, or some other substance into energy

Watergate scandal   the events that led to the resignation of president Richard M. Nixon; it began with a burglary at the Watergate Hotel in Washington, D.C.

SELECTED BIBLIOGRAPHY

Dolan, Edward F., and Margaret M. Scariano. *Shaping U.S. Foreign Policy: Profiles of Twelve Secretaries of State*. New York: Franklin Watts, 1996.

Flocken, Carissa. *U.S. Presidential Motive Profiles and the Cabinet*. New York: Columbia University Journal of Politics and Society, 2014.

Gates, Gary Paul, and Dan Rather. *The Palace Guard*. New York: Harper & Row, 1974.

Grossman, Mark. *Encyclopedia of the U.S. Cabinet*. Santa Barbara, Calif: ABC Clio, 2000.

Johnson, Gerald W. *The Cabinet*. New York: William Morrow, 1966.

Keithly, David M. *The USA & the World*. 10th ed. Lanham, Md: Rowman & Littlefield, 2014.

Stahr, Walter. *Seward: Lincoln's Indispensable Man*. New York: Simon & Schuster, 2012.

WEBSITES

Inside the White House: The Cabinet

www.whitehouse.gov/photos-and-video/video/inside-white-house-cabinet

See photos of where the cabinet meets and take a virtual tour.

The President's Cabinet

www.factmonster.com/ipka/A0775305.html

Quiz yourself on the dates each department was added to the cabinet!

Note: Every effort has been made to ensure that the websites listed above are suitable for children, that they have educational value, and that they contain no inappropriate material. However, because of the nature of the Internet, it is impossible to guarantee that these sites will remain active indefinitely or that their contents will not be altered.

Published by Creative Education and Creative Paperbacks
P.O. Box 227, Mankato, Minnesota 56002
Creative Education and Creative Paperbacks are imprints of The Creative Company
www.thecreativecompany.us

Design and production by Christine Vanderbeek
Art direction by Rita Marshall
Printed in China

Photographs by Alamy (J Marshall/Tribaleye Images, Niday Picture Library, North Wind Picture Archives), Corbis (Bettmann, Corbis, GraphicaArtis, Jeff Vanuga), Creative Commons Wikimedia (E. Anthony/Brady's, Jocelyn Augustino/FEMA, Albert Bierstadt, Brady-Handy Collection/Library of Congress, Bureau of Engraving and Printing, Eric Draper/U.S. Federal Government, Ralph Eleaser Whiteside Earl/The White House, Samuel G. Heiskell, jacobolus, C. E. Lewis/Library of Congress, The Obama-Biden Transition Project, Gilbert Stuart, John Trumbull/Washington University Law School, U.S. Department of State, U.S. Federal Government), Getty Images (Peter C. Brandt), iStockphoto (Maxim Anisimov), National Archives Catalog (War Department/Office of the Chief Signal Officer/Series: Mathew Brady Photographs of Civil War-Era Personalities and Scenes, 1921-1940), Shutterstock (elenabsl, Everett Historical, Kapreski, Ikeskinen, Pensiri)

Library of Congress Cataloging-in-Publication Data
McAuliffe, Bill.
The Presidential Cabinet / Bill McAuliffe.
p. cm. — (By the people)
Includes bibliographical references and index.
Summary: A historical survey of the presidential cabinet, from its beginnings to current structure, including its executive role and influential members such as Salmon P. Chase.

ISBN 978-1-60818-673-0 (hardcover)
ISBN 978-1-62832-269-9 (pbk)
ISBN 978-1-56660-709-4 (eBook)
1. Cabinet officers—United States—Juvenile literature.

JK611.M43 2016
973.09/9—dc23   2015039271

CCSS: RI.5.1, 2, 3, 8; RI. 6.1, 2, 4, 7; RH.6-8.3, 4, 5, 6, 7, 8

First Edition HC 9 8 7 6 5 4 3 2 1
First Edition PBK 9 8 7 6 5 4 3 2 1

Pictured on cover: Madeleine Albright